AF371713

Memoirs of My Divination

Misty Dawn Shakti Sharma

ISBN: 978-1-61244-900-5
LCCN: 2020918012

Halo Publishing International, LLC
8000 W Interstate 10, Suite 600
San Antonio, Texas 78230
www.halopublishing.com

Printed and bound in the United States of America

To my soulmate, Vikas. I love you forever.

To my sons, Brandon and Hunter.
I know unconditional love through you.

To soul. To love. To the infinite potential.
To the divine. I am forever loved
and forever remembered.

Contents

Longing

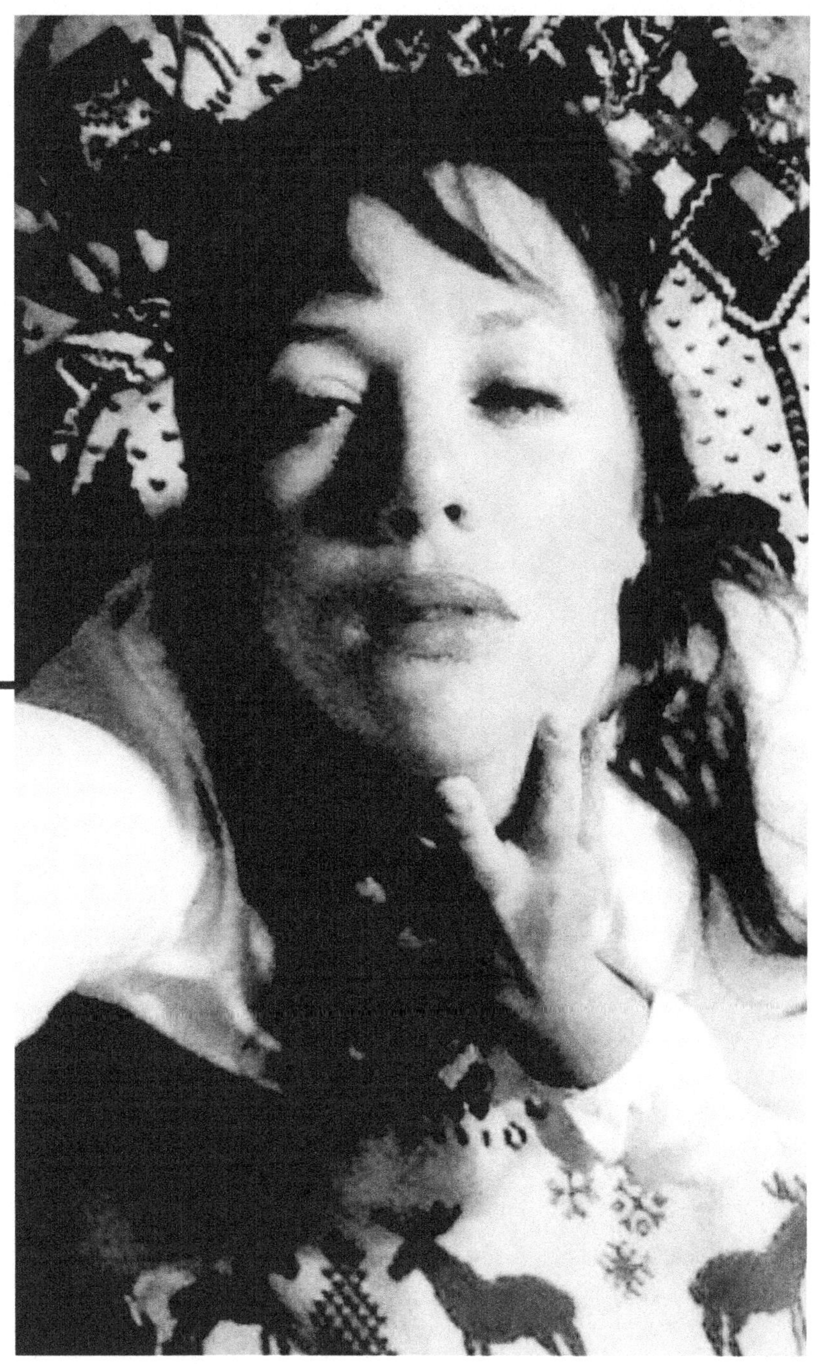

I felt a small cry in my soul. It came after so long. I had been fighting, you see. Fighting to make something of myself. Fighting to break free of so many attachments, so many energies. I did not realize how much I was begging for love. How lost I really was. I desperately held on to what was not meant to be mine. So many people around me sucked from my energy. They were cruel. And my heart hurt. My soul fled deep inside, battered a bit. But I always remained hopeful. Always when I needed it, spirit showed itself into my life. And a longing remained. A longing to journey deeper into discovering the soul I am. Longing for a healing. Longing to journey into the mysteries of the universe. I wanted the universe to reveal itself to me. I was searching outside of myself for completion, happiness, and retribution.

I was surprised to find I was the mystic, the great sage of my own life, of my own destiny.

I began awakening the goddess within. Shakti rose from my spiritual spine. And I shook with life.

Come flow with me on my journey. It has pain, sorrow, and hope—so much hope. And most importantly, it has love. For to love is the soul's greatest work here on Earth and in every dimension.

As you journey into my journey, may it inspire you to awaken your own soul.

May you begin to ask yourself what it feels like to be home.

May it inspire and heal. May you feel love.

May it wash over you.

My hope is that you know you are not alone. You are loved, so deeply loved.

PRESENCE

Here I am, my love. Why do you wait, hesitate?
Where are you?
I am ready.
Are you near?
Will you call?
Will you come?
Darling, please…please…

Nectar of Love

I want to drink from the nectar of love. To not be consumed, but to be upswept. To not pine or crave, but to feel the exponential expansion. To breathe it in throughout my being. To feel it coursing through my veins, as much a part of me as my blood.

And alas, this is how I love, how I breathe, and how I feel now that I am open and have allowed love through my doors.

There is no closing. There's just this ever-opening bliss. Every day I'm awakened, renewed, pure, and raw in this divinity.

My Love is Like This. This is My Love

My heart cannot help but to cry out and sing for you.

I tell it to calm itself, that you are not ready to take a risk for love, but it will not listen. It does not care.

The societal norms, ethics, and morals I have guarded so near. My heart says you are not my ruler, for I have no ruler.

I am not bound by time.

I am boundless, infinite, grand, divine.

I have tried to contain my love, but it cannot be kept or contained or fenced in. It is wild and free and grows of its own accord.

My love is like this. This is my love.

Pulsing Rhythmic Song

I had no right to stare at your hands and try to memorize the lines, to notice they were rough yet soft. The nails had a little dirt beneath, and I could not help but wonder what it would feel like to be that dirt, soft and cool beneath your fingers, molded into something grand by your hands. I had no right to press my lips to your hand and cover my heart, but I wanted you to feel the beat you create in me, the pulsing rhythmic song only you inspire. You fell back, eyes wide, from the force of my love. I did not mean to intrude upon you. I only meant to show you a little of what you do to me. I am sorry. I am sorry. I had no right.

LONGING

I let go of longing.I cried and cried.
It was like saying goodbye to a not-so-great friend, but one who held the space nevertheless.
Where that empty space was, the one that longed and pined, it has now healed. There is no pain.
It has expanded, and in that expansion a fear started to rise: a fear of not knowing what would fill that space.
And then, amidst the tears and fears, the answer came.

Love.
All there will ever be, all there ever was, and all there is now is love.
Love of myself and others infused in the place where longing had resided.

SAFE

You are a safe place to be, to dream and be free
of life's limitations and barriers.
The barriers that were within me have lifted,
and I am reborn.
I can close my eyes without fear, without control, without reason, without expectation.
You are a safe place to be.

Holy Love

How messy.
How grand.
It wakes me in my sleep in the dead of night and awakens with me in the early morning rays.
It is with me, as much a part of me as my breath.
It is holy, non-contained, expansive, big, and beautiful.
It grows, and none of your words stop it.
It is there, ever ready. It will not be denied or ignored.
You can pretend it does not exist, but I have to feel it, because you see, I am it, in my purest form—just like you are in your purest form—love.

Burning Hope

I burn. I burn for you.
You said to hold it, create it, love.
I did, but you hold it like a carrot dangling, spoken but not given.
You let me burn, so high and long.
I'm breathing in the smoke of this flame.
It started in my heart, in the core of my love, and the flame fanned out, touching every part of me, burning my soul with fire, passion, pain, and pleasure.
I am blackened by the smoke until it clears and runs red with my impassioned blood.
Now it is white, pure.
Let me burn. Feel me burn for me, for you, for them, for love, for life, for truth.
I will scream and open and throw my head back and laugh at the beautiful, messy everything. You see, I am love.

Peak of My Moon

You are hot.
You are smoldering.
You have penetrated the core of my sun.
You have breached the peak of my moon.
You have grabbed my love.
You are holding it now, so be careful. Be careful, my love.

Piscean Love

You! You!
Why can't you?
Your reasons. Your logic. I am done. I can hear
no more.
Here I am with my open heart. There you are,
closing it.
You talk a lot of talk.
Bashing my water. Clinging to your misery.
But I am water. I move graciously, beautifully.
I am expansive like an ocean wave, the tide.
You can move with me or be swept up in my
tide, but you will feel me.
I am powerful love and devotion.
I bared my love, my soul, before you, laid it
bare and bloodied and raw.
I have never done that, been so brutally hon-
est. It felt good. It felt really good.
Until the outcome I never thought or imagined
would happen.
You said I could create, do anything.

I thought about it. I want it real good.

Stop denying and lying, punishing yourself and me in this self-deprivation.

You said I could have it, but you denied yourself and therefore me.

Wear your robe. Wrap it around tight. After all, you are just a boy, and I am just a girl, and this is just this.

I asked for a divine love. I thought this was you and me.

I let you go.

But I cannot get rid of the love, nor do I want to.

It has opened me. I am so open.

I am breathing, releasing big, beautiful breaths, and my chest is out, cracked open.

I cannot shove the love back in.

I will not apologize for loving you.

I cannot be polite and proper. The systems, morals, and ethics I clung to with every fiber of my being have been released.

There is just love, and I do not think it knows right and wrong.

I just want love. Is that so hard?

I do not want to be you. I am me, beauty and love.

Soul Immersion

I want to feel every inch of you pressed upon me. I want your hands to mold me like clay until I am shiny and alive, like I know only you can make me.

I want to taste your lips and your soul, to know your intimate warmth.

I want to entangle everything I am around everything you are, until we move and rise and breathe and love as one.

One body. One light, moving, breathing, seeing, and loving.

Heart Terrains

My heart needs many terrains: soft, sweet, firm, and kind.
And you, my dear, are all.

CRICKETS' SONG

I lay on the cold green grass, staring at the dark velvet sky. Our limbs were entangled, wrapped around each other.
I had never felt this way, had never known I could give and receive yet still be whole.
As I lay with my head on his chest, I heard his beating heart, and our rhythms matched and, I felt, *So this is love.*
Sleep came quietly, softly, as I listened to our breathing and the crickets' song.

Love Pieces

You are unlike anything I have ever known.

You have captured me.

You are the hole puncher, and you punched a thousand little pieces out of me. You pocketed them by your breast, forever capturing me and my love for you.

I can never escape, and though it is lonely here, sometimes, occasionally, you free my love and let it swirl in a cascade of light and love all around us, encasing and enrapturing all we are and all we know.

Moonbeam Roses, Firefly Thoughts

Lay me down on a bed of roses. Whisper your love in my ear.

Show me your love with hands, lips, and the feel of your beating heart beneath my palm.

Believe with me in love, in life, in the moon and the stars.

Believe that the sun's rays will play against our skin, illuminating our hopes and thoughts.

Blaze with me under the sun, in the cool green grass.

Run with me like the wind blowing all around, aimless but happy, idle but purposeful.

Dance beneath the canopy of stars. Hold me in your arms tightly, warmly, under the coolness of the moonbeams, in a world all ours.

Heartbeat

I wish my hands were your hands so I might feel the touch of you and you might feel the flesh of me.

I wish my heart were in your chest so you might feel its erratic, pulsating beat, which beats for you when you are near me.

I wish my lips were yours so you might taste the passion they bear.

I wish my soul were yours so you might see the core of me and you entwined in love.

Rose Woman

Hold me in your arms a thousand nights, a
span of a lifetime.
Love me openly, freely.
Do not condense me or you or this.
Expand. Feel it expand.
I opened my heart. I bore forth all my love.
Do you feel it?
Does it scare you?
Will you run?
I am a rose woman. Mayhap I love too strong,
too bold, but this is me. I will not change.

Moon Peak

Can you love me at the highest peak of my moon, at the burst of my dawn?

Can you worship me and be devoted unconditionally while still providing safe harbor, so that I will not question the security of your love? So that I will feel its grip through all time and space?

Will it wrap around me, not just my body or thoughts? But will it coil around my heart, my soul, until all we are is woven together and spread on the blanket of all time, of all eternity?

Primordial Cry

That I would let out a cry so deep from my soul,
my heart, and my being, the world would not
question it, nor would I question the power of
my being to go on always, never ending.
And would you answer that cry, my lord Shiva,
with one to match?
Would you rise to meet me there among the moon?

Love Letter

I sat down to write you a love letter, but I could not find the words to write.

What words existed to describe your beauty? I knew none.

What songs could express your magnificence? None sprang to mind.

And so I wondered what existed to express the beauty of you. How could I capture the essence of you?

I realized then that I could not, for you are meant to be free, and the only way I can express the beauty of you is the love I feel in my heart.

Eclipse

Come to me, my love.

I need you so.

My heart is beating to the sound of your soul.

I need to feel your touch.

I need to know your taste, the sound of your sweet kiss.

The warmth of your eyes.

The protection of your arms.

My love, wrap me up, hide me away in your love for a while, and bring me out when our worlds are aligned together.

GOLDEN LIGHT

I am not built to stay at shore,
harbors anchor-heavy.
I am the wind, the wet water.
Deep down within, where my blood and
bones and dreams all mix, is a longing so great,
so intense, that it moves the world.
The sun feels my heat and graciously loves me.
Its rays of golden light penetrate.
The moon knows my magnetism and deeply
roots within my core.
The soil feels my rains and absorbs the wet
moisture of my love.
The oceans feel my waves crashing at their
shores and kindly take me in, whitewashed in
sea foam.
All of this because I long for you.

CHORDS

You spark the chords of my soul.
You dance on the waves of my mind, a vision
not part of time.
My heart opens. My spirit soars when you call
my name.
Can you feel me in the spaces between your day,
when night falls for you and dawn rises for me?
Do you feel the thunder of my love?
The loud crackling of my desire?
Do you feel my worship, and will you always?

Shakti's Penance

When I think of you, my whole body shakes. My energy rolls. Everything is heat, like Shakti doing penance for Shiva to show her devotion. It's the same for me. The world shall feel the heat of my long burn for you. I burn on and on… Slow…liquid…love.

Down within… Deep down within is me, myself, my light, my purity, my essence.
Here I fell into myself. I cracked open, and a lotus heart bloomed, fragrant and beautiful in color. Now I stand before you, goddess in bloom. Should I not be impatient for our coming together?
For goddess knows the stakes of life, of love. No day is promised. Should it not frustrate me to want you in my arms now?

So I stand before you not just as a goddess, but as a woman deeply yearning to be filled.

Will you fill me in all the ways only you can?
Will my lord Shiva answer my deep heart
songs? Will he sing back with his magic tongue?
Will we come together so that even the sun and
moon shall remember their birth, their coming
into being?

We shall sing such glorious songs!
And the cosmos shall rejoice that we have come
together again.
Our love, so pure like water.
Divinity remembered among the reuniting of
our hearts.

I ache! I long! I burn so high and so low! I dance!
I sing!
I am a human in love.
I am love.
Love.

INDIA

Waking up to your messages was the best. You mean everything to me.

I feel so blessed to share your love. You are the most beautiful spirit.

I love your soul, your strength, your tenderness. The way you talk and think. The way you love. You move me to tears, the beauty of you. Half of my heart is here with my children, and half is in India with you.

Awakening

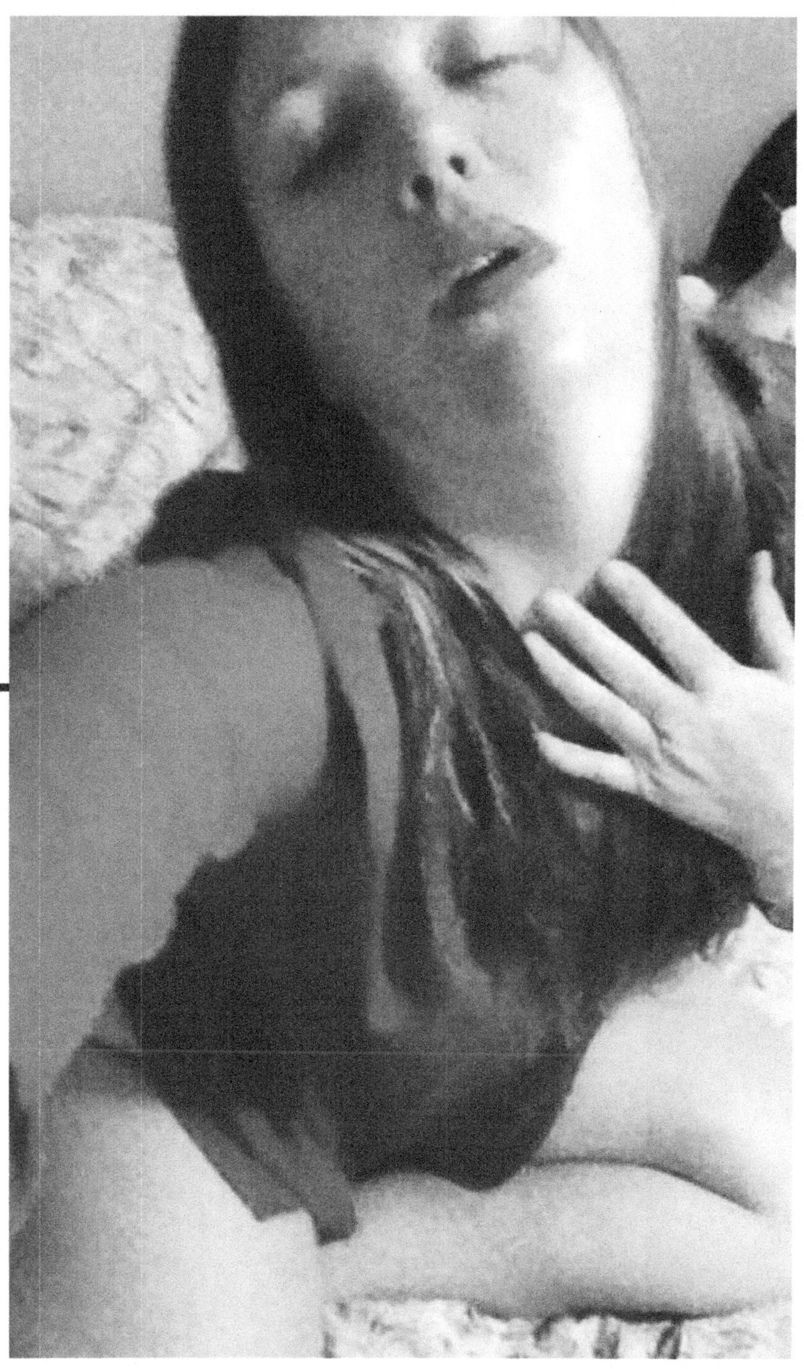

I came alive. The spaces within myself were released. Like a dirt field, cleared of all the roots and trees. Anew. I was like this for a time. Emptied, exposed, unsure, raw. All of the many things and moments and memories that had packed these spaces were now gone. I could breathe again, deeply. After a while, I sowed my own heart spaces, which became fertile ground for the infinite planting of spirit. Divinity shined in my center. Light had entered me. God had entered me. I opened again and again. I felt myself flying with the divine. Everything looked different. The sky, the moon… all welcoming me back with new eyes. I talked to the trees and manifested by the moon. Water my portal. The mud beneath my feet became my heartbeat. I lost myself as I journeyed deep into the unknown. I found myself gently held, being rocked by the great Shakti, mother. I learned to soothe myself, to hold myself, to love myself again.
This gentility I am.
This love I am.
This hope I am.

Spiritual revolution never comes easy. It will bend you and try to break everything you know and hold dear.

Clinging… We cling to everything.

Let it go, the soul whispers. But still we cling until the death of ego occurs, and then the silence comes.

Ascension has its price, complacency be damned. I am uncomfortable, but I am opening again and again and again.

The contractions of spirit expanding, quaking. I have no clarity.

I can barely see in front of me. Just enough to try to keep my balance.

But why? It seems less to fall.

Silently, I will pick my heart and soul back up, for mine is to bear what mine is to bear.

I do not know where the path is going, and yet I trust myself.

Have you ever felt exposed? Have you ever felt changed within your core and all the way out? What did it feel like? Journey with me deeper into my awakening, and may you be open to allowing any feelings, thoughts, or emotions to flow, grow, churn, and move you. May you find the love you may be longing for within.

WISDOM

I greet the moon as an old friend, the bare earth before my feet as my mother. I gain strength and wisdom from walking soundly. The stars are my compass. The sun, my golden light of warmth and love. The mountains are my fortitude, never wavering, always pushing up and on. I lost myself within the earth and found myself again among its beauty, until I realized I am all that I am: earth, moon, sun, mountain, and beyond.

SPELLBOUND

You have cast your spell on me. I am bound.
No return for my soul.
I looked into your eyes and remembered times
from long ago.
Now I am dancing in the rain. I am dancing in
the whirlwind of my life.
I feel! I feel! I feel everything!
The pain, pleasure, comfort. I behold you from
afar and near. You are inside me and all around,
woven throughout. Your breath excites me.
Your smile entices.
Your eyes penetrate me to the very core, until
I am nothing but smithereens of what I was.
I stand tall, head held high, with my arms out-
stretched, all my love pouring out.
And I do not care who sees or knows that I
love you.
You have me on my knees, suspended in
time, with no place to run, no place to hide.
All there is here is love. It has expanded and
overcome any other emotion, any other sense.
How do I move forward with this?

Heart Push

It is not a broken heart; it is an open heart. The difference is that a broken heart is awash with ego, admitting a defeat of love and spirit. An open heart is just that: open, beating, breathing, moving, and loving, without thought, ego, or reciprocation.

Naked Love

I am feeling open and raw, like all of my insides are exposed, especially my heart and my love. There is a part of me that wants to crawl back inside myself and wrap around myself so I am safe.

But I cannot go back.

I can only keep on reminding myself to breathe and stand tall and open.

This openness is so vast, so uncontained, only filled with the love that has caused the expansion and vastness.

And so I am back to how I came in my original form: naked love.

REBIRTH

I have watched all of the layers I built around myself be stripped away.
I have felt the tearing and opening, the rebirth-ing of my skin, of my soul.
I feel everything in its natural form. The ego is gone. Momentarily, it peaks, but there is no need for it here among the love.

Sugar, Wild, Woman

You are arrogant, proud, stubborn, and set.
Principled.
So devoted to your fight.
Am I so wrong?
Is this not right?
I complicated that pretty existence. I muddled
it up, soiled it with my love.
But some like misery, I forget. Some like misery.
Not me!
I will not crumple, and I cannot be broken, so
don't even try.
I am wild and free!
I am woman!
I am everything!
I am back from the long sleep, awakened and
free.
Touch me.
Grab my face and press your lips to mine.
Run your fingers through my hair.

Lay me down, swept up in you, in me, and in
this beautiful poetry.
Touch me. Love me.
Free this passion. Do not make me set it aside.
It is too good.
It cannot be tamed.
It is wild, free, and sugared with everything it
can be.

New Soil

My heart is new soil, freshly turned and fertile.

Goddess Bliss

Goddess is in full bloom, pushing past every notion I have ever held spiritually, emotionally, physically, mentally, and sexually, and it feels like an expansive bliss.

Soul Remembrance

I am being led through worlds not always my own.

FATE

You changed my life, or maybe I did.
I felt fate pushing me along, and I knew I was
arriving at something.
Something that would change my life.
Whether that was you or me, I no longer know.
This mirror is reflective, and every time I see
you, I am rushed headlong into the truth of
my core, of my gut, to the blackest depths of
my being.
And I have stood smiling, complacent, and
calm, just taking whatever you could give.
Little comforts that I mean something to you.
I cannot manipulate, control, or force.
I know these things now, but can I wait?
Can I love and let go?
Can I continue to be me? Alone. Raw.
Unfiltered.
Can I find balance and harmony and hope
without longing?

These are the questions I am living.
What are you living?
What are we breathing?
I know the sound of your voice; it is like heaven all around.
Your touch heals and soothes.
Your eyes…I am lost in their depths.
Time has stood still, collapsed, and yet it is moving along at full speed, and I do not know if I can keep up.
I beat myself up over and over again, until I'm not sure whose voice is speaking.
The only constant I have is love.

Lotus Love

Come here.
Come near.
I feel you in all the parts of me.
I feel you even when you are not near.
And when you are near, I run like warm liquid,
melting, soft and churned, ready, pliant. Like
the lotus, every day I break free through the mud
and blossom anew for you, for me, for love.

STAYING OPEN

I will let you fade into the darkness.
Without a word. For what are words, anyway?
In a time. In a moment.
Whispered. Ushered into the nothingness of
promise, of passion, of devotion.
"Why?"
Was never easily asked or answered, and yet
here I am, again asking, "Why?"

"Why do you open your heart again and again in
a world that constantly tries to shut it down?"

I have no choice but to open it. I can never go
back. It is.
And so it is, and so am I: love.

MOON

I send a wild call to the moon, you see, because
she is me.
I wake with her.
Sleep with her.
I cry out my dreams to her ears.
I bleed with her.
I birth with her.
I die and am reborn, MOON.

WILD

I am shrouded in all that I am. You cannot break me away now that I have tasted the wild.

Now I am free to roam the depths of my own soul, to sink into the inky warmness of my own depths.

Be careful with the steps you dance around my soul. I run deep, and you may not return the same as you were before.

CRESCENT

Crescent…The smoke billows around me. I swore I would not let it smother my love, my voice, my soul.

I realized then that the smoke was me, moving against the air, rhythmic, expansive, sleek. I had never felt so good as then, that alive feeling of grinding my hips to the image of you.

DIVINE

That feeling when you want to climb so far inside yourself, to feel the warmth of your own heart, your own soul…that is how you know you've opened. You are raw. There is no place to shut it in. You remain open. You are divine.

DIVINITY

I sat before myself, eyes wide, heart beating, open.
There was no preparation for divinity, and yet
there was a slight remembrance.
I touched my face to know I was here, alive,
present.
My eyes.

RAW FORM

I was born into this world a writhing, crying, naked being.

I am still a writhing, crying, naked being.

But in the moment I felt your pure love, my soul absorbed by you and yours by me, I knew the meaning of entering the world as raw as you and me.

To feel so deeply is like nerves all exposed, and there were times we bled, cried, and screamed out our sorrow like the wolf howls at the moon.

Who could hear?

Who could know?

Where are you?

Where are you, my beloved?

Here you stand before me.

Your spirit and essence familiar and warm.

You have wrapped yourself around me, coiled into my being.

I now cannot remember a time before. I know why I entered the world a writhing, crying, na-ked being; it was for you.

Awakening

I have sat with the broken. I have been the broken myself.
My heart has known betrayal. My soul has known loss.
I have grieved and begged.
I have danced with fear and sung in defeat.
I have held life within my womb. I have held love throughout it all.
I have lived in love, even in my darkest moments.
I have awoken to life.
I have awoken to love.
And it is there, in love, that I knew god is in me and in you.

Memoirs of My Divination

I delved deep into the unknown. Here it felt scary and beautiful, like the dark, inky depths of the soul.I felt myself breathe for the first time, knowing my breath was sacred.

I am not my name or my body. I am nameless yet infinite.

I felt myself sinking deeper into these truths.

I am one.

I am whole.

I am the cosmic dance, the eternal male and female.

The grace.

With these truths, others held faded away. This felt like death.

Like a tornado, ripping apart my soul.

What was left?

My heart was now fertile ground for the infinite planting of spirit.

Every breath tender.

Every sound and touch penetrated.

I was newly born. I felt a humming, a deep, primordial rhythm.

My heart was beating again.

All of myself felt alive, connected, joyous, orgasmic, divine.

I got down on my knees in prayer and cried joyous, rapturous tears of gratitude.

Thank you!

Thank you!

Thank you, divinity!

In me, of me, beyond and within.

I stretched my back and lifted my breasts, my chest, my heart toward the sky.

Ahhhhh, the feeling that awoke. From where, I did not know.

I only knew the shaking vibration of my deep inner soul and core.

I let the feeling come again and again and again. It shook me. It took over me. I was and I am divine.

I am tall like a tree; my roots are deep.

I sink into the earth and cover myself with soil. My blood is so cool, so wet, so life giving.

When I am dry, I come here.

The mother's milk never runs dry. Always, she is fecund.

I opened my mouth, my heart, my yoni, my soul, my words, and my depths to the divine.

I arose, newly born, an infinite being, rapturous, golden, liquid, permeable, and ready to move my soul on Earth.

I felt so big, so enormous.

I was cracking thunder, turbulent wind, burning sun, and long, liquid, pale shining moons.

Glorious, Glorious, Glorious!

I sang fevered prayers from wet lips.

I danced passioned quakes and shakes.

I screamed again and again, "I am alive!"

I am alive.

I have remembered!

I have remembered! I am infinite!

I am raw, soul incarnate.

Here and now is my Eden, my grace, and I grabbed your hands and let my burning passions catch flame.

Healing

A longing lead to an awakening of my soul. A massive healing occurred. An ebb and flow of release and growing. Healing is not always light. It can feel dark, scary, and unknown. The greatest challenge was who to talk to about this journey. Could they feel or understand? There were people and teachers. Sometimes real, but sometimes found within the pages of my internet searches. I wanted to understand every experience I was having. I sought knowledge and words so I could understand. I learned the gift of how much I feel. This is not a curse; it is a gift. I learned to allow this internal feeling to guide me, heal me.

Negativity spreads likes poison, infecting those around. Perceptions are distorted. Fear clouds judgement. Love prevails over all.
I choose love.
I will not fear.
My perceptions are clear. I am pure in my heart. I need not prove to you, or you, or you.
Just me.
Let go.

I learned to listen to the soft stirrings of my soul. I learned to love myself as I would a newborn, tenderly and with such care. I had forgotten how to love myself, how to hold myself. I felt such healing at learning to love myself again. And I let myself flow into this. I massaged my skin and took long baths. I took classes and went to new places just because I wanted to. I was not afraid to wander. To explore. To cry. To sit. To feel wonder.

As you read through my healing, allow yourself to open. To feel the possibility of love. What it feels to hold yourself so dear. May you have the heart to explore all the many moons of you.

Comfort Love

What is sleep?

Why is it needed when my ears long for your voice?

When my soul longs for yours?

When my body aches for your kiss, my energy dancing, waiting for yours to join? And so I find myself blessed. I am experiencing divinity through my humanness. I need not wait for ascension.

Such a blessing, and yet I must sleep, eat, live, and complete chores of the day.

There is beauty in this.

You say it adds to our love, and I feel what you say.

You are wise, progressive in thought, as your name suggests, but in this moment I would surely give much to hear your voice, to feel your kiss, and to dance with you along the shores of our souls.

My comfort is to close my eyes and focus on
feeling you. Only then can I fall asleep, know-
ing we are wrapped together in our love.
I think it beautiful to be loved so good, and
you have loved me so good.

Om Shaktima

When Shakti is alive in you, every moment is a dance.

You begin to walk with a new breath, a new wave of pulsating energy.

You cry out in the ecstasy of the gift of life.

Your lips part to taste the air. Your arms open to take in the love, and your heart outpours more and more. You realize then that life is a love frequency, pulsating, dreaming, and dancing with you.

Love is its flame, its source.

When you realize this, you begin to truly live life.

Om Shaktima.

Burning inside, deeply longing, for the world does not recognize love.

Still, love is my god, my hope, my religion, my faith.

Love is all I pray.

My tears are rolling. They are hot, liquid, fiery prayers on my fevered lips, murmured in my shaking bliss.

Love is all I know.

Om Shaktima.

Velvet Gaia

I dreamt I saw myself, and I was there, the earth gleaming with moss.

I was so green, covered inch by inch.

I spread out into a mass of deep, shaded trees with roots more ancient than myself.

I felt the rich, dark soil filling my veins.

I had been so empty for so long.

The river trickled slowly into my open, waiting mouth. I could feel the nourishment of my own divinity within. I was deeply rooted in the here and now.

I spilled over into the moist green ground again and again, never depleted, the sun filling my core. Here the rain fell, and I basked in the glory of that wetness, the intimacy we shared.

I had lost my soul and body, but I remembered them among the earth.

And now, when you look at me, there is confusion in your eyes, for you see I am the raw, naked, bleeding being bared before your veiled eyes. That black veil. That cursed veil you refuse to remove.

But alas, my dance is not to change you. My dance is an ancient rhythm, one you can only know after you have swum the deepest currents, throbbing in terror, desperation, and fear. Currents that broke through barriers of deep, abated longing. Longing that held faith in love, and faith in love that brought forth fruit. Glorious fruit of many labors.

Now, when you look at me, mayhap you see a wild woman, drenched in the gleaming green moss, covered inch by inch. I fly.

CORE

I am the fires of the deepest of Earth's core in your love.
I am the deepest, wettest, darkest waves of the ocean, crashing again and again, when you touch me.
I am the sun's light from head to toe, bursting into golden rays, lighting up my soul, when you love me.
I am my purest, brightest, hottest in your love.
Feel me, my divine love.

WHOLE

I touched my bare hands to the naked earth
and felt the beat of my soul.
I looked up into the face of the moon and felt
whole.
The pulsating vibrancy of life beating within me.

Gentle

Let me wake easy. Do not rush this love.

SELF-LOVE

There is something about a woman falling in love with herself.
The way her face looks. The way her body sways.
The heart opening. The inner smile, knowing that no matter what, she has herself.
She holds herself so dearly, so gently.
Forevermore.
No longer searching outside.
Her walls all down. No fortress now.
She knows she has held it all within herself, just waiting to touch, to open, and to love herself again.

Magic Love

And in a moment, she let herself breathe into all it meant to be alive.

Woman, light, and love.

She let herself fall without worrying who would catch her.

She let herself dream, dance, laugh, and cry.

She let herself be.

And she found she was love.

Love was there, breathing into her. Love was there to catch her. Love let her dream, dance, laugh, and cry.

She screamed with joy when she realized she was love.

Endless, timeless, magic love.

Winds of Time

It matters not to me the size or strength of your arms, just that they are open and can hold me, as they have and as they will.

It matters not the color of your hair, for no matter the color, you will always be beautiful in my eyes.

It matters not your past, just that you stay present with me.

All that matters to me is that you love me openly, devotionally, and with kindness.

And do not worry about my love, darling. It is steady, strong, and consistent. It will never waver. It will stand all tests of time.

I found solace in your arms.

In your warm embrace.

In the way your eyes hold mine. In the way your lips have spoken my name.

In the way our hearts came home with each
other forevermore.

Like a soft wind, you came to me. Your
warmth. Your touch.
You opened your arms, and I could breathe
again, forever found.

SELF

I wish you could see you are worthy of the love you deny yourself.

Free from the guilt you pile on high.

Released from the shame carried for generations.

Rid of the hate cast upon you by a society that only sees your sex, your body, your car, your job.

This is not you.

I see you.

I see your heart, your mind, the light you are.

You are beautiful, kind, loving.

You are deserving.

You are not alone.

And when you cannot see it, come back to me, and I will show you again.

For we started this journey together, and together we shall remain.

Love from yourself.

To My Beloved

You are my heart's whisperings.

My soul's deepest longing.

You are the earth, the wind, the moon.

The night and day begin with you.

Once I was burning, as were you. Like the stars burn, we were on fire, wild, aimless, and hurt. Now we are free in our love.

You are exploring the depths of me. You have entered deep down inside, where no one has gone. You saw me then, this soft, shy flicker of loving light. You held me in your warmth, and I knew love. I knew no more longing.

I knew only peace.

I glow more beautiful than ever before.

Held in your love, I feel my heart blooming, opening even more to you, to us, to our divinity. Let the world speak in all its many tongues. We will speak the only language we now know: love.

And when our many days have started to pass and the years have come and gone, our souls will depart for more unknown, held together, journeying deeper into love.

Ecstasy

You sang me into orgasm, the hot water touching me, my hot fluid inside growing warm, glowing, and mixing with the hot water.
The roses melting, the scent not as intoxicating as yours, my love.
Oh, my divinity. Oh, my love. How I love you.
How my blood sings!
My eyes are jeweled when they look at you.
My skin alive, a breath, a pulsating of its own to your voice, your touch.
I hold the secrets of the universe in my soul, my heart, my divine yoni, and I want to shower you with their blessings.

Reverberation of Love

Love is not bound or set by any species. It reverberates high among the jungle skies and low among the darkest soil.

It does not call to man or woman, rich or poor. It answers purely to soul.

Love knows no bounds. It cannot be held and coveted, kept wrapped and sound.

Love is the ever-moving pure essence, cracking open hearts again and again, overfilling the cup inside you again and again.

Till you scream out in pure joy, pure bliss, at the feel of divinity, at the feeling of what we truly are. Wrapping you sound in her arms, Ma is here.

Message from Divine Feminine Rising

Keep your ideas of perfection. I will kindly keep my own.

Do you think I can be broken? I am Shakti, she who runs deep in my blood and in my soul.

I am goddess.

Do you think she cries or cares if her thighs touch or her breasts are big and bouncing? Goddess does not have time for that.

Goddess knows life is not promised. She is busy making a life of love and purpose, grateful for the gift of body and the temple, though not obsessed.

I have bled.

I have shed my skin a thousand times, risen up after being beaten down, and I will again and again. And as I rise, I hold a hand to you.

Do you think I will cover myself because of your discomfort? I will laugh as I run in my glorious, naked form.

Hear me. I am goddess. Hear me. So are you. To rape me is to rape your soul, a damnation you wish to never know.

DEPTHS

Sometimes I sink deep down.
Down below breath.
The only warm depths, the spaces I used to
flee from, are now my saving grace, my harbor.
I have born.
I have born myself again and again. Bear wit-
ness to me anew, abashed, in golden perfection,
in dewy madness, my heart a living chamber,
my breath a reminder of all my love.

Rani

You make me feel like Queen Shakti, dancing on and on.

Covered in flowers, my heart spaces blooming again and again and again.

Oh, my love, you make me wild. I am dancing underneath the moon, my skin pale and aglow, underneath and above and surrounded by your love.

I am wet.

My heart saturated. Deeply. My heart is raining forth its deepest storm of rains.

It is ecstasy!

Ecstasy!

Ecstasy, to be loved by you!

Come take my hand, my love. Deeper and deeper, we will go into our jungle of love. Deeper into awareness and understanding of caring for the ancient and remembering divinity. Masculine and feminine unite in a cosmic explosion of infinite potentials nourished by love.

WATER

I never understood why the oceans rage, why the relentless waves crash again and again.

Now I know why the ocean crashes again and again, white sea foam hitting cliffs, the sky cracking with thunder, bright flashes of love in the sky.

Again and again, they come, no matter how tired, how sore, how sad, how mad, how frustrated, confused, lost… Again and again, those waves come forth to the shores.

For you see, the waves love the shores, and I know this because I am the ocean, and you are my shore, maybe just out of reach.

But again and again, I'll come, my dear lover, because I long to feel my water mix with your warm white beach.

Carrying me on to depths I have never known. Feel me, my god, my king, my love, my divinity.

I am crashing and leaping and dancing and rising up, up, until at last I explode in water, dripping, touching you like I have before.

Loving you like I have known you before.

Finally, I have reached you again.

I know this rhythm, and no one can take it from me.

It is you and me.

And we shall know all the mysteries of the world through love.

DESERT WOMAN

I know the desert, the dryness.

Lying in the blackness, my mouth is so dry.

My body is tired, pressed with warmth and heat, wet from sweat.

When I drop the cool liquid water down my mouth, I am refilled. Love is like this, too. When you are dry, when you are weary, and when you are at your last moments of life, let love flow gently through you, rejuvenating your very soul. Every drop is life giving. Every drop of love nourishes your very core.

Nymph

Once, I was a fairy who danced like a nymph, naked and gleaming before the full moon, orgasmic in my joy, my bare feet kissing the earth. My ancestors are the trees, and I can still feel my roots buried deep in the earth, the coolness caressing my veins.

The soil rich and dark and deep and satisfying.

I drink from the earth's springs, cool and bright.

I dance again.

I dance again.

Manifestation

When following your dreams, you will be feared, hated, loved, celebrated. Follow them anyway.

The soul dies in small ways by not trying for change. Never give up.

I began to speak mantras and affirmations. Once I had control of my thoughts, it became easier to manifest. I would release by the full moon, writing down what I felt no longer served me and asking to release it. I would write down what I would like to manifest by the new moon. I would speak in present language, as if it was already occurring, and I would think in this way, as well. I was consciously thinking of planting these thoughts. Imagining what may grow. I was journeying deeper into the mysteries of the universe within me.

I prayed. I moved my body through dance, and I ran when the emotions became too strong. I kept within me a hope. I loved my children. I went to work. I worked on myself again and again in a million different ways.

My heart ached. And there were days I did not know how I would go on. But I manifested my hopes, my longing, my love. I manifested my life, my healing, and my self-love.

Whatever you imagine is possible. Whatever you tell yourself, you become. These are truths. What do you dream? What do you want to manifest? Is there something you need to release?
What are you planting and growing in your own soul? In your life?

VISUALIZATION

I sat on the edge of my bed and began to run the brush through my hair.

I closed my eyes, pretending it was my lover, my great lord Shiva.

After a moment, it was no longer my hand moving. I was still.

I looked up to see my lover there, his dark eyes branding my soul.

I let out a breath, and he inhaled it.

And so our dance began, no longer breathing as two but as one.

He circled behind me, and I felt him lift my hair. He came close, smelling the roses I had bathed in. His lips brushed my neck, and I let out a cry.

Slowly, without rush or a purpose to finish, he gently brushed my hair over and over, again and again.

Each time, I thought he would tire, bore, or finish, and yet he continued on and on. Finally, when I knew no start or finish between him or me, he turned me to face him, and I was struck to my core by the love I saw shining back at me.

No words were spoken, and yet, in that simple gesture, I learned that every act is an act of god.

When we touch ourselves or others. When we bathe, eat, sing, or dance.

And I awoke to this. I danced feverishly and with wild abandon, for I remembered my truth, my place, my divinity.

Sometimes I cry out for my lover. I am not quite sure where he is, so I continue to love myself in his absence.

I have learned to love myself so good. So good.

Manifestos

When I am dreaming, I am me.
I am listening, for in the dream world, conscious and subconscious merge languidly.
I am fully connected to my divinity, to yours, and I turn manifestos of my spirit into rising action.
I heal.
I am rebirthed from the womb of myself again and again.
Ah, the gift of dreams.

Soulmate

Do I dare dream that you are Eden, that we shall rise in all the ways the cosmos had intended and then still continue to rise?

That we shall burn with our longing on and on? For our shared divinity? For our coming together? I open and long and love each day with this dream, until it takes such root in our souls that it becomes and transcends into all we know.

I dare to dream that I shall have my lord Shiva in the flesh.

Emanate

Learn to massage your own skin. Learn to love your own heart, mind, body, and spirit.

Allow this to emanate from your every fiber and in your every word, thought, action, and movement. Love yourself deeply, and when the hands, heart, and soul that love you like you love you come, open yourself up as wide, high, and far as possible and let everything shine and be. Allow yourself to be loved deeply, as alas, you have learned what love is.

Incarnate

I cannot blame myself for wanting to hear you
and feel you again.
I am goddess free, and you god free.
Still, I am flesh and blood woman, with desires
and fires you rouse within.
Do not deprive me or you, of what feels so
good, so right.
Lie down upon my lips. Hold me as you say
you will in our rapture, our bliss.

Persevering Love

He is coming.
I can feel it in my heart, within the beautiful, sacred space created with the flurries of excitement and love.
I am here, open and ready to create in this life and love, my sweet love.

Heady

I followed the moon as it danced on the shores
of you.
Oh, how the light danced off your beautiful skin.
The touch of you. The feel of you.
The sight of us wrapped together.
I basked in the moon's light as I basked in the
love you gave.
I let myself sink deeper into the feeling of you.
Deep, deep, deeply flowing.
Until we became liquid, warmth, hot and
heady, on and on and on.
I knew not the beginning of time, space, or
body, but I knew the beginning dawn of love.
Love me as only you can, deeply and tenderly,
securely held in your heart space. Wrap me up
into you. Carry me away in your love.

SMILE

You made me smile.
It was simple.
And yet it spoke to a place deep within my heart, a place maybe that needed to open…just a little more.
I cannot forget you finding joy in my joy.
You entered my heart then.

SEARCHING

I was a wanderer, a vagabond.

My heart had been torn, my soul burned.

I knew not what would come. I just held on and let go, too, deeply knowing I had always had this ache, this drive to find you.

And when I least expected, you came, my heart's deepest desires alive before my eyes.

You love me in all the ways I prayed for.

When I had balanced myself, I was okay alone, and yet my soul let forth these achy screams all hours of the days. Howling, my soul searched for you, relentlessly scanning the earthly planes.

And now you are before me, the most beautiful. You were worth all the pain, sadness, and uncertainty. Worth the fight to keep my love and hope.

That is what you are, my love. You are my hope, my love.

You are the long day and the slow, burning night.

You are my brightest sun and the highest peak of my moon.

There is no ending in your eyes. I see only my future.

For you have me, all my love, every breath, every heart space. You even have my soul.

I lay myself before you in complete love, complete devotion, and faith.

My love, let me kiss any hurt or anger you have suffered. Let me pour my love all inside you, so that you rise like the moon, new and shining in my love.

I will keep you safe with my love and watch over you. Watch you rise and soar. The two of us together, like a phoenix rising to meet the moon.

Our past, that long time of yearning, is ashes, and now we are reborn together in our shared love.

Vikas

And in the feel of your love, I became as a bird, freer than I had ever been, singing sweetly for you.

The clarity came then, upon the meeting of our souls.

We knew why we had entered the world as writhing, crying, aching beings.

I knew not how to impart to anyone other than you what that ache felt like. No matter what I did, no matter where I went, and no matter the love I held for self, still I ached and burned for you.

Now the ache has been replaced with the love you feed me and the love I feed you.

And we are feeding and pouring and dancing and singing together.

You are my great love story.

You are the hope I held in the dark when the world asked, "Do you dare to open and love once more?"

I smiled then at the world, at all who called me a fool. I smiled through tears, loss, and death. I smiled as I remade myself into my purest form of raw love, and I smile now as I stand before you.

I smile because you are the physical, mental, spiritual representation of hope and love that I held.

To behold you, to look into your eyes, and to feel your energy pouring into every piece of me, heart spaces opening, love entering deeper and deeper into each other.

I know love.

I thank you.

I know what it feels to be loved deeply and purely.

I know love.

You sang to my heart. We laid our souls bare.

Our energies meeting again after who knows how long.

How I glow from you.

How our love flows inside, radiating for all to see.

This is what it looks like to be loved. And oh, how it feels.

To be loved as I love.

COMPASS

I think the moon loves the sun.

I know this because it is the same way I love you.

Each day, when the sun sets, she rises, lighting the sky with her love, looking for her lover.

The sun rises, and she is in another time, still loving, still feeling the sun.

We say we know the location in space of our sun and moon, but I only know you.

You as my compass, my light, my time, my existence.

Across time and space and energy and love, I searched for you.

It has sometimes looked and felt like a sad love because of the physical distance between.

Always cycling, patiently hoping, and believing when many would give up.

But the patience and hope are what brought me to you.

What happens when the sun and moon meet?

A love so great it changes the world. A love so true is lasts infinitely. And on and on.

I love you, my hope, my love, my Vikas. Looking forward to our infinite journey.

TENDER

You held me softly.
You looked into my soul.
You drank my tears. You knew what they were for.
You loved me deeply, my body and my soul.
I realized then I had barely known love.
When you kissed me, the world stopped. It turned liquid. No time existed. There was just you and me and the beginning of creation.
I love you.

Soul Kiss

And then he took me in his arms, and I knew.

I looked up and saw the moon, and she saw me and said, "I told you that you would be loved because you are love.

I have seen you in all your many lifetimes, and when your faith has wavered, the one constant that always brings you back is love."

I looked into his eyes, the moon reflected in them, and it felt so good, so warm, so right to be wrapped snug in his embrace.

He lowered his mouth to mine, and I felt sparks of beautiful energy opening and blending, the taste of him all around me, and I held on for dear life, lost but found in this intoxicating love.

Do not ever bring me down from here!

And then he laid me down and cradled my head and heart in his hands so tenderly. His kisses were everywhere now: my mouth, my neck, and my cheeks. And I cried tears of joy!

Of love!

Of being alive!

And he allowed these tears. He knew what they were for, and he kissed them right up as we flowed and glowed in our beauty.

He kissed my very soul, and I let him.

I opened!

I came undone!

I was raw!

And he loved me up, and I loved him out, until we rose with one beat, one heart, and one soul forevermore.

And then the sparks came, and it felt like millions of lights cascading from our love.

Soft, Steady Love

And my skin came alive for you.
My heart was touched so deeply at its core.
It began a new beat.
Rhythmic in its dance.
Loudly beating its joy and desire for you to hear.
Is love so powerful that it can reroute a sad heart?
I pondered.
And at that moment, you kissed me so deep,
so sweet, and my heart leapt in response. *Yes,*
I thought, *love is powerful.*

Softly held in the warm darkness of you, basking in the light of the waxing moon, I bared
witness to your soul and you to mine.
Not a gentle opening, but a grand leap of love
and faith.
I was content in your arms, surrounded by the
warmth and the steadiness we create.
I felt the hum of our hearts, our souls dancing
along together.

MOONRISE

I was on the porch swing, watching the moon rise, the sounds of crickets in my ears.
The only lights, the moon, and a few fireflies who came to hear my tune.
They heard my song, my fervent prayer, a soul's salute to love.

Transmutation

Internal transformations from the inside out are always the hardest, the rawest. Like being gutted and opened in a way you have never opened before.

They are also the most beautiful.

If you cannot see miracles, you will not experience them.

If you cannot see the divinity in yourself and others, you will never have divinity here and now.

If you fear change for yourself or others, you will never know the infinite possibilities of creation.

When you love people, you allow them to be free, wild, raw.

The soul can never be caged.

At our deepest depths lives a will to live, to adapt, for the human spirit to evolve in, and evolve we shall.

When we come to love, and when we allow it to rain over every aspect of our universe, we will then know immortality.

I am a star moon traveler. From far away, I come. I know I am dancing moonbeams and light fly.

Allow yourself to be transmuted across space and time. How do you feel? What does your world look like? Who are you with? These questions can rock your soul and change your destiny.

LIGHTWORKER

They asked what are you?
Who are you?
Where are you going?
I said, "Love."
I am it.

Planetary Rotation

If we came together, the world would stop, tilt, and spin on its axis, and the sky would be the ground. The moon would be my floor.
I would be covered in the flow of you.

SUNCATCHER

My skin needed to travel the world to feel the sun at different points.
The colors of different skies, cascading all around, until I fell in love with all that was and all that would ever be.

Adaption Creates

I am exploring all the facets of you, down into the deep darkness of nothing, of something, of possibility.
There I found a mirror and was surprised to see myself reflected before my very eyes. The flaws, my ego, stripped, laid bare.

I am not the same, you see, nor will I ever be.

I had to grow, expand, change.
For what happens to any life when it cannot adapt?
It surely dies.
Though once I felt darkness, struggle, a net of fear wrapped around me, I have allowed the light within me to implode and burst forth, shattering anything but love, hope, and faith.

And so I am free, for I love openly, unabashedly, without shame or gain.
Not to win or lose or take.

But to give.
To enjoy the god within you.
The taste. The touch. What our love feels like.
We are the creators!
Love: our lifetime masterpiece, sometimes patched together with threads, sometimes strong and sturdy like oak, and sometimes fluid like the sea, but always it is there beneath the surface of all that was and all that is.
Wake up and remember!
Have you forgotten?
Remember. Remember.
You are, and have always been, and always will be absolute, wonderful, simple love.

Gossamer Substance

When I sleep, I dream of you, for I long to be free with you and you with me.

No words need to be spoken, and yet they would flow like golden liquid from our tongues, dancing in the dance of all time, covering us in the beautiful gossamer substance of our love.

There we would bare all, open all, share everything we are and the possibilities of what we could be.

We would not scoff at each other's otherness; we would just warmly embrace each other's ways of being in love.

We would know love, for we would be love in its purest form: unconditional.

That is my hope for us.

That is my dream.

I Am

There is a wisdom in my bones.
A wisdom in my soul.
It knows far more than I know.
If only I listen. If only I feel through the pain,
the discomfort, the breaks.
I shall know I am.

Timeless Space Love

Sometimes I am at a loss when I try to explain why I stay open. Why my heart beats not only for me but for all of you.
Why I look at the world and smile.
Why I love a little more every day.

But then I am brought to my knees by something, falling down in gratitude.
I am bared open once more, cracked to the core of all I am, was, and all I have the potential to be.
It is here in this place that I love, for it is all I have left to give, to receive.

Love crosses all space and time. Any moment that we spend in love is a moment in which we live forever.
It is timeless.
It is you.
It is me.

Nataraja

Oh, great Shakti and my lord Shiva, you mate
on the depths of my soul.
You have come together again, and I am for-
ever changed.
I am feverish, writhing, dancing in your con-
juring, for I am you, me, we.

That primordial dance of all existence breathing
through my breath. Come through me. Now it
is my choice to live.
And I shall know the dance of all dances, the
song of all songs, reunited at last.

Transform

I learned to speak to my body as kindly as I did to my children or my lover, and I watched it transform before my eyes!

Blessed Are the Lovers

Blessed are the lovers, for they know time, distance, and space as illusion.

Love is their only constant, raising them to depths only barely discovered, the infinity of creation spanned before their hearts. Pure in the love they exchange, they rise higher, exalted in the highest of high.

For to love is to know god and goddess and all of creation.

To know one's own infinite potential and bathe it in love, then share that love, is to go on and on. One is free from suffering, from burden. One has found Eden.

RED BURNING LIGHT

If you were the night, I would turn black.
If you were day, I would be light.
If you were water, I would be your liquid, infused throughout your being.
If fire, I would burn red, hot, slow, and long.
Because you are you, I am all of these: black night, light, water, and fire burning red, hot, slow, and long.
For it's you I love.

Liquid Silk

Make me forget my name, and remember only
I am goddess alive, breathing, heart beating
fast for you.
Whisper your desires into my soul, my heart.
Let all be known between us. Leave your reservations before you come to me. There is no
need for them at the gates of my sweet love.
Can you feel me?
So warm. Such heat as I burrow myself into
your spaces.
Will you answer, meet, rise to my wild call?
The moon hears my sweet cries. Will you?

I sit before you, bare.
Can you feel my heart space opened?
Can you feel my mind open?
Can you feel my body opening?
Can you feel my energy, like satin, liquid, warm
silk flowing from me to you, from me to you,
from me to you?

Ah, I felt you feel. Ah, I feel you opening.
Do not fear me.
Dance with me among the stars.
Let me show you the moon.
Breathe in the smoke of my love. Feel it fill your lungs. Be rejuvenated by my touch, by my golden, liquid love.

Hold me.
Touch me.
Kiss me a thousand times, and then a thousand more.
Weave me into you, in all the spaces we are or will ever be. On and on…

ETERNAL FLAME

Should I hang my head because I have loved
and lost?
No!
I will not.
Shall I feel shame?
No!
I will not.
Remember me for all I am.
Always willing to open again.
Always journeying deeper into the wild depths
of love.
You can venture here to meet me or move out
of my way.
Either way, you will feel me burn long and
slow, my eternal love a never-ending flame.
Grow warm with me, or dance in my shadows.
I am a force of love.
I cannot be stopped.
For love is all there really is.

MUSICIAN

You have such command over my instruments:
my heart, my body, and my soul.
How your words reach out lightly yet deeply
strum me inside.
The music you create within my deep, wom-
anly womb. My deep, honeyed nectar flows
for the sound of you.
Our symphony rising, wrapped in darkness
that is sweetness guided by the moon, we
howl. There is no beginning, no end, no birth,
no death. Just love.

OPEN

In your love, I was set free. No past. Only our present. Only this future.

There were many things that told me not to love, not to open one time more.

I refused to listen.

I opened again, wider each time.

I now know why.

Clarity has come.

I have continued to open through all things in my life: pain, sorrow, sadness, anger, confusion, and fear.

I opened so I would be wide enough to feel your love, for your love is like mine: big, expansive, and full of purity. And now your love is inside me.

I transform. I open even more so this love falls in a beautiful waterfall all around me, soaking each and every thing, each and every person, refilling endlessly.

Our love is a gift, a beautiful example to the power of love, hope, and faith.

I love you, my sweet Vikas.

You are my eternal love, the flame burning within my soul.

Arambha

And I know how the world came to be. Out of the darkness, two souls became one. The longest, sweetest kiss that bloomed a millennium.

I saw you there before me. The mountains, the air, and the ocean crashing again and again at my feet, knocking down the walls of my heart.

I lie before you, my arm the root of trees, my breasts the rays of sunlight dancing to your lips, my back and bottom valleys, my yoni endless rivers, my mouth with yours the gate of heaven. I know how the world came to be, my love.

Raw Angel

I am not of this world. I am a visitor, here to love. My angels asked me before I came, "Are you sure you wish to go feeling so deep? It is going to hurt."
I answered, "Send me raw."

Rhythm

I am dancing with divinity, flames of desire
licking at me, reminding me of my source.
I twirl. I dance. I sing. I am joyous!
I remember this is my state of grace: love.
Do not drag me back! No!
You cannot.
This is where my heart and soul stay.
Like a paper you let loose in the wind, I am
a soul with no direction, free, endless, wildly
dancing upon the hope of a fleeting moment.
Love me.
Do not try to understand.
The soul, divinity, and love all must be felt.
Come. Grab my hand and dance under the
moon while the wind gathers and showers us
in her love.

Kavi Heart

I need not go anywhere, for right within me are the mountains, the milky, snow-covered Himalayas.

Deep within me are flowing rivers, like the Ganga, racing fast, slow, pulling deep, deep, deep. Washing me clean, the sun sweetly kissing the droplets from my flesh.

The grasses of the meadows are where I lay my head when I am weary. The softness and the intoxicating breeze of wildflowers renew my soul so deep.

The richest sands of the hottest deserts flow in my Kavi heart.

My deepest waters form an oasis, where the lotus blooms, dark-soiled mud all around, covering my wounds.

I am Earth mother, safe and sound.

I am green and full of life-giving.

The moon is my temple. At night I climb, sometimes crawling to her steps. There I step into her cool glow, her cool breeze. There I manifest my love.

Sometimes I am like the ocean, calm, softly swaying, sweetly cooing my motherly sounds. And then, deep within, my Kali Durga rejoices, and the rich molten liquid of my passion forms. My passions wash over me, you, our souls, and our life again and again.

Do not fear the time passing, for we have forever. I will love you forever.

Night falls after the sun has risen. I kiss the forehead of my sweetly sleeping sons. To know love, to love, and to be loved. I have lived. I am immortal now.

Phoenix

Growing takes time. Every time I think my soul complete, I am growing again. New skin, soul, mind, body, spirit.

Like the phoenix, I crumble in ashes daily, only to be renewed by the flames of love that slowly lick at my patched-up heart.

My spirit glides then, like the birds I see in the sky, so weightless. Weightless. Fearless. Fearless. My hope, my faith, and my love save me daily from death, the mind-blowing death that occurs to soul.

I am here, grounded in the roots of my spirit, dancing in the ocean waves, covering myself in the thick black mud of life.

My lotus heart bursts through the mud, gleaming golden, sparkling. I forget sometimes as I am wrestling with life. I remember that's a choice, too, to try to wrestle and control instead of flowing through the endless rocking waves. I have gone under a few times, only to burst through, gasping for my life.

My life, my love, my dream.

Always, my spirit will soar. Like the phoenix, I rise from my ashes again. I cannot be contained. I am divine spirit rising.

Cosmos

Cosmic, darkness, glowing, radiating.
Moon dust, star beams.
Liquid energy.
I am ascending to dimensions unknown. No
fear. Gladly, my crown glows.

Made in the USA
Monee, IL
07 July 2026

56550099R00095